ANCIENT ROMAN LAW

The Twelve Tables
and
The Charter of Urso

by

Unknown Ancient Roman Patricians
and
Emperor Julius Caesar

ISBN-13:
978-1973858065

ISBN-10:
1973858061

Table of Contents

Forward

These are two of the earliest written forms of Roman law; which dating back thousands of years. Interestingly, you'll note that many nations laws are based in early Roman law. Even today, the similarity between current United States laws and early Roman laws is astounding.

The spelling of words and punctuation appear as they are in the original Tables.

Mike Rothmiller

THE TWELVE TABLES

Introduction to the Twelve Tables

Following Roman tradition, it is believed the first ten Tables were written by a commission of ten men of the Roman noble class. Later, another commission consisting of twelve men was assembled to complete the final two Tables in roughly the years 451-449 B.C..

In 449 B.C. the Tables were ratifed by the Centuriate Assembly and were engraved on twelve Tables which were displayed on the Rostra before the Curia in the Forum of Rome for all to read, understand and obey.

The Tables stood as the foundation of Roman law and the Roman Constitution.

These laws were the result of long standing tensions between the patricians (the ruling class) and the plebeians (the ordinary citizen).

The commoners demanded rights and finally achieved some.

The Twelve Tables

Table 1

1. If anyone summons a man before the magistrate, he must go. If the man summoned does not go, let the one summoning him call the bystanders to witness and then take him by force.

2. If he shirks or runs away, let the summoner lay hands on him.

6-9. When the litigants settle their case by compromise, let the magistrate announce it. If they do not compromise, let them state each his own side of the case, in the *comitium* of the forum before noon. Afterwards let them talk it out together, while both are present. After noon, in case either party has failed to appear, let the magistrate pronounce judgment in favor of the one who is present. If both are present the trial may last until sunset but no later.

Table 2

2. He whose witness has failed to appear may summon him by loud calls before his house every third day.

Table 3

1. One who has confessed a debt, or against whom judgment has been pronounced, shall have thirty days to pay it in. After that forcible seizure of his person is allowed. The creditor shall bring him before the magistrate. Unless he pays the amount of the judgment or some one in the presence of the magistrate interferes in his behalf as protector the creditor so shall take him home and fasten him in stocks or fetters. He shall fasten him with not less than fifteen pounds of weight or, if he choose, with more. If the prisoner choose, he may furnish his own food. If he does not, the creditor must give him a pound of meal daily; if he choose he may give him more.

3. Against a foreigner the right in property shall be valid forever.

Table 4

1. A dreadfully deformed child shall be quickly killed.

2. If a father sell his son three times, the son shall be free from his father.

5. A child born after ten months since the father's death will not be admitted into a legal inheritance.

Table 5

1. Females should remain in guardianship even when they have attained their majority.

Table 6

1. When one makes a bond and a conveyance of property, as he has made formal declaration so let it be binding.

Table 7

1. Let them keep the road in order. If they have not paved it, a man may drive his team where he likes.

9. Should a tree on a neighbor's farm be bent crooked by the wind and lean over your farm, you may take legal action for removal of that tree.

10. A man might gather up fruit that was falling down onto another man's farm.

Table 8

2. If one has maimed a limb and does not compromise with the injured person, let there be retaliation. If one has broken a bone of a freeman with his hand or with a cudgel, let him pay a penalty of three hundred coins. If he has broken the bone of a slave, let him have one hundred and fifty coins. If one is guilty of insult, the penalty shall be twenty-five coins.

3. If one is slain while committing theft by night, he is rightly slain.

4. If a patron shall have devised any deceit against his client, let him be accursed.

10. Any person who destroys by burning any building or heap of corn deposited alongside a house shall be bound, scourged, and put to death by burning at the stake provided that he has committed the said misdeed with malice aforethought; but if he shall have committed it by accident, that is, by negligence, it is ordained that he repair the damage or, if he be too poor to be competent for such punishment, he shall receive a lighter punishment.

23. A person who had been found guilty of giving false witness shall be hurled down from the Tarpeian Rock.

26. No person shall hold meetings by night in the city.

Table 9

4. The penalty shall be capital for a judge or arbiter legally appointed who has been found guilty of receiving a bribe for giving a decision.

5. Treason: he who shall have roused up a public enemy or handed over a citizen to a public enemy must suffer capital punishment.

6. Putting to death of any man, whosoever he might be unconvicted is forbidden.

Table 10

1. None is to bury or burn a corpse in the city.

3. The women shall not tear their faces nor wail on account of the funeral.

Table 11

1. Marriages should not take place between plebeians and patricians.

Table 12

5. Whatever the people had last ordained should be held as binding by law.

THE CHARTER OF URSO 44 B.C.

Introduction

The Charter of Urso is also know as the Law of Julia and is believed to have been drafted by Julius Caesar. After Caesar's death, it is believed by scholars that Mark Antony enacted it as the law of the Roman Empire. In the ensuing decades, a variety of changes has been made to the charter.

Unfortunately, most of the charter has vanished over the centuries. It is assumed that the majority of copies were destroyed when Brennus, the leader of the Gaul's, sacked Rome in 390 B.C.

In 1870 and 1871 four bronze Tables were found near Osuna, Spain. In ancient times that region was known as Urso, Spain.

Most scholars believe this charter was the foundation of Caesar's Roman Law with much of it carrying over to modern law.

Interestingly, the connection between current American law and the Tables is stunning. If any, the people had little power. The real power remained in the hands of the Emperor, the Senate, other members of the ruling class and the wealthy.

As mentioned, only a portion of the Charter was found, that's why the items begun with entry 61.

Definition of terms in the Charter of Urso; A decurion was a member of a city senate in the Roman Empire. Decurions were drawn from the curiales class, which was made up of the wealthy middle-class citizens of a town.

Genetiva Julia was a Roman colony.

----

61. In the case of any person being commanded to lay hand on the said defendant: such laying hand on the same shall be on the legal ground of a judgment given, and it shall be lawful for the said person to perform such act without prejudice to himself. The surety shall be a man of substance at the discretion of the duumvir or other judicial authority. If the defendant fails to offer a surety or to obey the judgment of the court the said person shall lead him off. He shall keep him in chains according to the civil law. In the case of any person resisting by force: if he is convicted of the same he shall be liable to double the amount claimed and besides shall be condemned to pay to the colonists of the said colony 20,000 sesterces; and in respect to such money, any person at will shall sue, and the duumvir or the person charged with jurisdiction shall exact and shall adjudicate.

62. In respect to all duumvirs: each duumvir shall have the right and the power to employ two lictors, an aide, two clerks, two summoners, a copyist, a crier, a soothsayer, and a flutist. In respect to the aediles in the said colony: each aedile shall have the right and the power to employ a clerk, four public slaves in girded aprons,la a crier, a soothsayer, and a flutist. In this number they shall employ persons who are colonists of the said colony. The said duumvirs and the said aediles, so long as they hold their magistracy, shall have the right and the power to use the toga praetexta, wax torches, and tapers. As respecting clerks, lictors, aides, summoners, flutists, soothsayers, and criers employed by each of the same all the said persons, during the year in which they perform such services, shall have exemption from military service. And no person, during the year in which they perform such services for magistrates, shall make any such person a soldier against his will, or order him to be so made, or use compulsion, or administer the oath, or order such oath to be administered, or bind such person, or order such person to be bound by the military oath, except on occasion of sudden military alarms in Italy or in Gaul. The following shall be the rate of pay for such persons as are apparitors to the duumvirs:

for each clerk 1,200 sesterces, for each aide 700 sesterces, for each lictor 6oo sesterces, for each summoner 400 sesterces, for each copyist 300 sesterces, for each soothsayer 500 sesterces, for a crier 300 sesterces; for persons serving the aediles the pay shall be: for each clerk 800 sesterces, for each soothsayer 500 sesterces, for each flutist 300 sesterces, for each crier 300 sesterces. It shall be lawful for the said persons to receive the aforesaid sums without prejudice to themselves.

63. The duumvirs first appointed to hold office till December 31 shall have, each severally, the same number of attendants which is allowed by this law. And the said attendants shall receive not less than that amount of pay, which would be properly paid for one fourth part of the year, and the total pay received shall be proportionate to the duration of their service; and that amount it shall be lawful for them to receive without prejudice to themselves.

64. All duumvirs holding office after the establishment of the colony shall bring, within ten days next following the commencement of their magistracy, before the decurions, when not less than two thirds are present, the question as to the dates and the number of festal days, the sacrifices to be publicly performed, and the persons to perform such sacrifices. Whatever a majority of the decurions present at such meeting decree or determine concerning the said matters, it shall be lawful and valid, and such sacrifices and such festal days shall be observed in the said colony.

65. Respecting any money paid into the common fund under the category of fines in connection with taxes belonging to the colony Genetiva Julia: no person shall have the power to pay such money or to give or to attribute the same to any person, except for such sacrifices as are performed in the name of the colonists in the colony or in some other place; and no person shall receive such money for other purposes without prejudice to himself, and no person shall have the right and the power to make a proposal concerning such money to the decurions or to formulate a resolution. And the duumvirs without prejudice to themselves shall give and attribute the said money for such sacrifices as are performed in the name of the colonists in the colony or any other place; and they shall have the right and the power so to do. And it shall be lawful for the person to whom the said money is given to receive the same without prejudice to himself.

66. Respecting pontiffs and augurs created from the colony Genetiva by Gaius Caesar or by the person who by his command establishes the colony: such persons shall be pontiffs and augurs of the colony Genetiva Julia and shall have their places in the colleges of pontiffs and augurs within the said colony, under all the conditions and with all the rights appertaining to pontiffs and augurs in every colony. And the said pontiffs and augurs, having places in their several colleges, and also their children, shall have exemption from military service and from public duties solemnly guaranteed, in such wise as a pontiff in Rome has or shall have the same, and all their military campaigns shall be accounted as discharged. Respecting the auspices and the matters appertaining to the same: jurisdiction and adjudication shall belong to the augurs. And the same pontiffs and augurs shall have the right and the power to use the toga praetexta at all games publicly celebrated by magistrates and at public sacrifices of the colony Genetiva Julia performed by themselves; and the said pontiffs and augurs shall have the right and the power to sit among the decurions, when they witness the games and the gladiatorial combats.

67. All pontiffs and all augurs of the colony Genetiva Julia, elected or coopted, after the issuance of this law, in accordance with this law into the colleges of pontiffs or augurs to fill the place of persons deceased or condemned, shall have their places as pontiffs and augurs in such colleges within the colony Julia, with all the rights appertaining to pontiffs and augurs in every colony. No person shall be received or elected in place of another or coopted into the college of pontiffs except at a time when there are or shall be less than three pontiffs belonging to the colony Genetiva. Nor shall any person be elected in place of another or coopted into the college of Augurs, except at a time when there are less than three augurs belonging to the colony Genetiva Julia.

68. The duumvirs or the prefect shall conduct and notify the elections of the pontiffs and augurs provided by this law in like manner as by this law it is proper for the duumvirs to be elected, created, or replaced.

69. The duumvirs first appointed after the establishment of the colony, during their magistracy, and future duumvirs in the colony Julia, within sixty days next following the commencement of their office, shall propose to the decurions, when not less than twenty are present, that the money payable in accordance with the conditions of lease to the contractor or contractors, who have purchased the contract to supply all things requisite for sacrifices and religious acts, shall be assigned and paid to such persons. Neither shall any other matter be proposed to the decurions nor shall any decree of the decurions be passed until the money in accordance with the conditions of the lease is assigned and paid to the said contractors by decree of the decurions, provided that not less than thirty are present when the said matter is discussed. Whatever is so decreed, the said duumvirs shall provide that same shall be assigned and paid to the contractor or contractors, provided that they do not pay or assign the same out of that money, which in accordance with this law properly must be given and assigned for those sacrifices are publicly performed in the colony or in any other place.

70. All duumvirs, except those first appointed after this law, during their magistracy at the discretion of the decurions shall celebrate a gladiatorial show or dramatic spectacles to Jupiter, Juno, and Minerva, and to the gods and the goddesses, or such part of the said shows as shall be possible, during four days, for the greater part of each day, and on the said spectacles and the said show each of the said persons shall expend from his own money not less than 2,000 sesterces, and from the public money it shall be lawful for each several duumvir to expend a sum not exceeding 2,000 sesterces, and it shall be lawful for the said persons so to do without prejudice to themselves, always provided that no person shall expend or make assignment of any portion of the money, which in accordance with this law properly shall be given or assigned for those sacrifices which are performed publicly in the or in any other place.

71. All aediles during their magistracy shall celebrate a gladiatorial show or dramatic spectacles to Jupiter, Juno, and Minerva, or whatever portion of the said shows shall be possible, during three days, for the greater part of each day, and during one day games in the circus or the forum to Venus, and on the said spectacles and the said show each of the said persons shall expend from his own money not less than 2000 sesterces, and from the public fund it shall be lawful for each several aedile to expend 1000 sesterces, and a duumvir or a prefect shall provide that the money shall be given and assigned, and it shall be lawful for the aediles to receive the same without prejudice to themselves.

72. Respecting all money presented or brought to the sacred temples under the category of religious offerings and respecting any portion of such money as remains from the sacrifices performed in accordance with this law in honor of the god or the goddess, to whom any such temple belongs: no person by act, or order, or intercession shall prevent such surplus from being expended in that temple to which the said money is presented or brought under the category of religious offerings, nor shall any person expend the said money or cause the said money to be expended for any other object.

73. No person within the boundaries of the town or the colony or within the area marked round by the plowla shall introduce a dead person, or bury, or cremate the same therein, or build therein a monument to a dead person. If any person acts in contravention of this regulation he shall be condemned to pay to the colonists of the colony Genetiva Julia 5,000 sesterces and he shall be sued and prosecuted by any person at will for that amount. Any monument so built a duumvir or an aedile shall cause to be demolished and if, in contravention of this law, a dead person has been introduced and placed therein, they shall make the proper expiation.

74. No person shall construct a new crematorium, where no dead person has been cremated, nearer to the town than half a mile. Any person acting in contravention of this regulation shall be condemned to pay to the colonists of the colony Genetiva Julia 5,000 sesterces and shall be sued and prosecuted by any person at will for that amount in accordance with this law.

75. No person shall unroof or demolish or dismantle any building in the town of the colony Julia, unless he furnishes sureties, at the discretion of the duumvirs, that he has the intention of rebuilding the same, or unless the decurions allow such act by decree, provided that not less than fifty are present when the said matter is discussed. If any person acts in contravention of this regulation he shall be condemned to pay to the colonists of the colony Genetiva Julia the value of the said building and shall be sued and prosecuted by any person at will for that amount in accordance with this law.

76. No person shall possess within the town of the colony Julia pottery works or a tile factory of larger size than to produce 300 tiles per day. If any person possesses such works or factory, the said building and ground shall become the public property of the colony Julia, and any person at will shall have the right to claim such building and any magistrate charged with jurisdiction in the colony Genetiva Julia shall pay without malicious deception into the public funds a sum of money equivalent to the value of the same.

77. If any duumvir or aedile desires in the public interest to make, to dig, to alter, to build, or to pave any roads, dikes, or sewers within the boundaries belonging to the colony Julia, it shall be lawful for the said persons to do the same, provided that no injury is done to private persons.

78. Respecting public roads and footpaths within the boundaries assigned to the colony, all such thoroughfares, roads, and footpaths that exist or shall exist or have existed in the said territories shall be public property.

79. Respecting all rivers, streams, fountains, lakes, springs, ponds, or marshes within the territory divided among the colonists of this colony: the holders and possessors of such land shall have the same rights of access, carriage, and drawing of water in respect to the said streams, fountains, lakes, springs, ponds, and marshes, as belonged to former holders and possessors. In like manner the persons who own or possess the said land shall have legal right of way to the said waters.

80. In the case of public business in the colony being given to any person by resolution of the decurions: the person to whom such business is given shall produce and shall render an account of the said matter to the decurions without malicious deception as far as possible within 150 days next following his completion of the said business or his ceasing to continue it.

81. In respect to all clerks of the duumvirs and the aediles of the colony Julia, to be employed in making entry of public money and in writing the accounts of the colonists: every duumvir and every aedile, before the said clerks make entries in the public account books, shall administer to each in a public meeting, openly, in the day time, on a market day in the forum, an oath by Jupiter and the household gods, that they will guard the public money of the said colony, and will keep true accounts in a proper manner without fraudulent intent, and will not defraud with malice aforethought the colony by false entries. As each clerk so takes oath, the said magistrate shall cause him to be entered in the public books. Clerks failing to take such oath shall not copy the public accounts nor shall they receive the money or the pay customary for such service. Magistrates failing to administer such oath shall be fined 5,000 sesterces and shall be sued and prosecuted by any person at will for that amount in accordance with this law.

82. Respecting lands or woods or buildings given or assigned to the colonists of the colony Genetiva Julia that they may have public use thereof: no person shall sell the said lands or woods, or lease the same for a longer period than five years, or make a proposal to the decurions, or carry a decree of the decurions, whereby the said lands and woods shall be sold or leased otherwise than as aforesaid. Nor, in the case of the said lands and woods having been sold, thereby shall they cease to be the property of the colony Genetiva Julia. And any person using the produce of the same on the ground of such purchase shall be condemned to pay each year to the colonists of the colony Genetiva Julia 100 sesterces for every juger and shall be sued and prosecuted by any person at will for that amount in accordance with this law.

91. Respecting any person elected or appointed decurion, augur, or pontiff in the colony Genetiva Julia in accordance with this law: whatsoever decurion, augur, or pontiff of the said colony fails within five years to possess a domicile in the said colony or the town, or within a mile of the town, a domicile of such value that a sufficient pledge can be taken from it, the same person shall cerse to be augur, pontiff, or decurion in the said colony; and the duumvirs in the said colony in a proper manner shall provide that the names of such persons shall be taken oi the public lists of decurions and of priests; and it shall he lawful for the said duumvirs so to do without prejudice to themselves.

92. The duumvirs holding office in the said colony shall propose to the decurions concerning the dispatch of public delegations when a majority of the decurions of the said colony are present, and any decree, passed by a majority of those present at that meeting, shall be lawful and valid. In the case of a person elected to discharge a delegation, resolved upon in accordance with this law or by decree of the decurions passed in accordance with this law, failing to discharge the same: such person shall provide a substitute from the said order, in such manner as is proper by this law or by the decree of the decurions. If he fails to furnish such substitute, and for every occasion of such failure, he shall be condemned to pay to the colonists of this colony 10,000 sesterces and shall be sued and prosecuted by any person at will for that amount.

93. No duumvir appointed or created after the establishment of the colony and no prefect left in charge by a duumvir in accordance with the charter of the colony shall receive or accept, concerning public ground or for public ground, from a contractor, or a leaseholder, or a surety any gift, or present, or remuneration, or any other favor; nor shall he cause any such favor to be bestowed upon himself or upon any of his staff. Any person acting in contravention of this regulation shall be condemned to pay to the colonists of the colony Genetiva Julia 20,000 sesterces and shall be sued and prosecuted by any person at will for that amount.

94. No person in this colony shall adjudicate or have jurisdiction, save the duumvirs, or a prefect left in charge by a duumvir, or an aedile, as provided in this law. Nor shall anyone cause by virtue of such irnperium or authority any person to adjudicate in the said colony, except those persons who properly adjudicate by this law.

95. In the case of recuperators being assigned and failing to give judgment on the day commanded: the duumvir or the prefect, when the case in question comes to trial, shall order the said recuperators and the party concerned in the said case to be present, fixing a certain day for their appearance, until the said case is adjudicated, and he in a proper manner shall cause adjudication on the said case to be made within twenty days after recuperators are assigned and ordered to adjudicate. And he shall cause public notice to be served on the witnesses as to the said case, not exceeding twenty persons, being colonists or resident aliens, selected at will by the person who conducts the case. And he shall provide that the persons on whom such notice is served and whose names are included in the list of witnesses shall be present at the said trial. And in a proper manner he shall cause anyone, who knows or has head aught of the matters under inquiry, to declare his evidence, after taking oath, provided that not more than twenty persons in all are compelled to give evidence at any one trial. No person shall be compelled to give evidence against his will if he is related to the party concerned in the said case, as father-in-law, son-in-law, stepfather, stepson, patron, freedman, cousin, or any nearer connection by

blood or affinity. In the case of the duumvir or the prefect, who makes such claim for the colonists, failing to be present: if such absence is due to serious illness, or business connected with bail, or jurisdiction, or sacrifice, or funeral in his household, or purificatory rites ensuing thereon, or if he is detained by some magistracy or power conferred by the Roman people, then it is not the intent of this law that, in the absence from the court of the person conducting the matter, the allotment or the rejection of the recuperators shall proceed or the matter shall be adjudicated. In the case of a private person making the claim, and failing to be present on the proper day for the holding of the court, and not having been excused, when the case comes at the discretion of the duumvir or the prefect, on the ground that one of the aforesaid causes of absence had arisen, namely, serious illness, or business connected with bail, or jurisdiction, or sacrifice, or funeral in his household, or purificatory rites ensuing thereon, or that he is prevented from attending by a magistracy or power conferred by the Roman people: then no action shall lie in respect to matters for which an inquiry is provided by this law. And in respect to such matter: the law shall take its course and the matter shall remain exactly as though no judices had been elected and no recuperators had been assigned for the said matter.

96. If any decurion of the said colony demands of a duumvir or a prefect that a proposal shall be made to the decurions concerning public money, or fines, or penalties, or concerning public grounds, lands, or buildings, whereby there may properly be made an investigation and an adjudication, then the duumvir or the person charged with jurisdiction, on the first available day, shall consult the decurions on the said matter and shall cause a resolution of the decurions to be made, provided that a majority of the decurions are present when such matter is discussed. Whatever a majority of the decurions then present determine shall be lawful and valid.

97. No duumvir and no person with the power of a duumvir in the said colony shall so act, or so propose to the decurions, or so cause a decree of the decurions to be made, that any person shall be a patron or shall be adopted as a patron to the colonists of the said colony, save the person invested by the Julian Law with the right to give and to assign lands to the colonists, and the person who established the said colony, together with their children and descendants, except after a resolution of a majority of the decurions present, passed by means of voting Tables, not less than fifty being present when the said matter is discussed. Any person acting in contravention of this regulation shall be condemned to pay 5,000 sesterces to the colonists of the said colony and shall be sued by any colonist of the said colony at will for that amount.

98. In the case of performance of any public work having been decreed by the decurions of the said colony, a majority of the decurions being present when the said matter is discussed: it shall be lawful for such work to be performed, provided that in any one year not more than five days' work for each adult male nor more than three days' work for each yoke of draught animals is decreed. The said public work by decree of the decurions shall be superintended by the aediles then in office. They shall provide that the work shall be performed, as the decurions resolve, as long as no labor is required, without his own consent, from any person less than fourteen or more than sixty years of age. Persons possessing a domicile or an estate in the said colony or within the boundaries of the said colony but not being colonists of the said colony shall be liable to the same amount of labor as a colonist.

99. Respecting any public aqueducts brought into the town of the colony Genetiva: the duumvirs then in office shall make proposal to the decurions, when two thirds of the same are present, as to the lands through which an aqueduct lawfully maybe brought. Whatever lands a majority of the decurions then present determine, provided that no water is brought through any building not constructed for that purpose, it shall be lawful and right to bring an aqueduct through the said lands, and no person shall do aught to prevent an aqueduct from being so brought.

100. In the case of any colonist desiring to conduct waste water into his private property and coming before a duumvir and demanding that the matter shall be brought before the decurions: then the said duumvir of whom such demand is made shall lay the matter before the decurions when not less than forty are present. If a majority of the decurions then present resolve that the waste water shall be conducted into private property the said person shall have the right and the power to use the said water in such way, provided that no injury is caused to private individuals.

101. No person holding the comitia for the election or by-election of magistrates shall accept at the said comitia any person for a tribe, or return or order the return of any candidate, to whom any of those causes attaches, whereby it is not proper or lawful for any person within the colony by this law to be nominated or created a decurion or to sit among the decurions.

102. No duumvir holding an investigation or conducting a trial in accordance with this law, unless such trial is by this law bound to be concluded in one day, shall hold the said investigation or conduct the said trial before the first or after the eleventh hour of the day. The said duumvir also, in respect to the several accusers, shall give to the chief accuser the privilege of making his accusation for four hours and to every subordinate accuser for two hours. In the case of an accuser conceding a portion of his time to another person: he shall give to the said person to whom such time is conceded by so much the longer time for speaking. He likewise shall give to the person who concedes a portion of his time to another person by so much the shorter time for speaking. For whatsoever number of hours in all the whole number of accusers have the privilege of speaking in each several suit he shall give to the defendant or the persons pleading for the defendant the privilege of speaking for twice the said number of hours in each suit.

103. Whenever a majority of the decurions present at any meeting determine to draft armed men for the purpose of defending the territories of the colony, it shall be lawful, without prejudice to themselves, for every duumvir or prefect charged with jurisdiction in the colony Genetiva Julia to draft under arms colonists, resident aliens, and "attributed" persons. And the said duumvir or any person placed in command of such armed force by the duumvir shall have the same right and the same power of punishment that belongs to a military tribune of the Roman people in an army of the Roman people; and he shall exercise lawfully and properly such right and power without prejudice to himself, provided that all acts performed are in accordance with the decree of a majority of the decurions present at the said meeting.

104. Respecting all boundary roads or crossroads, made or marked within the territories of the colony Genetiva, and all boundary ditches within the land, given and assigned by order of Gaius Caesar, dictator and imperator, and by the Antonian Law and by decrees of the Senate and by plebiscites: no person shall have the said boundary roads or crossroads blocked, nor have any heaps or obstructions therein, nor plow over the same, nor block nor obstruct the said ditches, whereby water may be hindered from running and flowing in its proper course. If any person acts in contravention of this regulation, for every several such act, he shall be condemned to pay to the colonists of the colony Genetiva Julia 1,000 sesterces and shall be sued and prosecuted by any person at will for that amount.

105. In the case of any person declaring that a decurion is unworthy of his place or of the order of decurions on any ground except that such decurion is a freedman, and in the case of demand being made of a duumvir that an action shall be granted concerning the said matter: then the duumvir, to whose court application is made on such matter, shall take cognizance thereof and shall grant an action. If the said decurion is condemned in the action, he shall cease thenceforth to be a decurion, nor shall he declare his vote among the decurions, nor shall he be a candidate for the office of duumvir or aedile, nor shall any duumvir at the comitia accept his candidature in the voting, nor shall return nor shall order the return of such person as duumvir or aedile.

106. No colonist of the colony Genetiva, established by order of Gaius Caesar, the dictator, shall organize any assemblage or meeting or conspiracy in the said colony.

123. In the case of a majority of the judices, before whom the said matter is treated, not being convinced that the person concerning whom the action is granted is unworthy of his place as a decurion: then the duumvir, to whom application is made on the said matter, shall order the accused person to be acquitted in the said action by the said judices. The person so acquitted, provided that no action is granted on the ground of collusion, shall be acquitted in the said action in accordance with this law.

124. In the case of a decurion of the colony Genetiva accusing of unworthy conduct another decurion of the said colony Genetiva in accordance with this law and causing in accordance with this law the condemnation of the person so accused in the said action: then the accuser, if he so desires, shall be allowed by this law to declare his vote in the place of the person so condemned; and it shall be lawful for the said person rightly, legally, and duly so to act without prejudice to himself, and the said place for declaring or demanding votes among the decurions shall belong by this law to the said person.

125. At the games no person shall occupy any plate given, assigned, or left to the decurions, from which it is proper for decurions to view the games, except the one who is at that time a decurion of the colony Genetiva, or who holds at that time a magistracy or authority or power by the votes of the colonists or by the command of Gaius Caesaz dictator, consul or proconsul, or who at the time has some promagistracy or power in the colony Genetiva, or to whom it is proper for places to be assigned among the decurions by decree of the decurions of the said colony, suda decree being passed when not less than one half of the decurions are present at the discussion. Nor shall any person, with malice aforethought, introduce or order to be introduced into the said place any others except the aforesaid persons. If any person with malice aforethought occupies such places in contravention of this law, or introduces another person into the same, or orders with malice aforethought another person to be so introduced, for every such act against this law, he shall be condemned to pay to the colonists of the colony Genetiva Julia 5000 sesterces and any of the colonists, at will, shall have the right and the power to bring an action, a claim, and a suit for that amount of money, in accordance with this law, in a

recuperatory action, before a duumvir or a prefect.

126. Every duumvir, aedile, or prefect of the colony Genetiva Julia, or any other person of the colony Genetiva Julia, celebrating dramatic spectacles, shall accommodate the colonists of the colony Genetiva, resident aliens, guests, and strangers in such manner as the decurions decree and determine, without malicious deception, not less than fifty decurions being present when the said matter is discussed. Whatsoever is so decreed and determined by the decurions shall be legal and valid in accordance with this law. Nor shall the person celebrating the games accommodate the aforesaid persons, nor order the same to be accommodated otherwise or in other manner, nor give, nor apportion, nor assign places, nor order places to be given, apportioned, or assigned in another manner, nor shall he do aught nor order aught to be done, whereby the said persons shall sit otherwise or in another manner than in the places to be given, apportioned or assigned, nor whereby any person with malice aforethought shall sit in a place reserved for others. Any person acting in contravention of this regulation, for each and every other act, shall be condemned to pay to the colonists, at will, shall have the right and the power to bring an action, a claim, and a suit for that amount of money, in accordance

with this law, in a recuperatory action, before a duumvir or a prefect.

127. Respecting any dramatic spectacles in the colony Genetiva Julia: no person shall sit in the orchestra to view the performance except a magistrate or a promagistrate of the Roman people, or a Roman official charged with jurisdiction, or a person who is or shall be or has been a senator of the Roman people, or the son of such senator, or the overseer of the workmen of the magistrate or promagistrate holding the province of Farther Spain, or Baetica, or those persons who properly by this law shall sit in the place assigned to the decurions. Nor shall any person introduce into the said place nor allow to sit therein any persons other than the aforesaid persons.

128. Every duumvir or aedile or prefect of the colony Genetiva Julia, severally during the year of his magistracy or imperium, as far as possible, in a proper manner and without malicious intent, shall provide that directors shall be appointed for chapels, temples, and shrines in such manner as the decurions resolve, and that the said directors, severally in each year, shall provide that games in the circus, sacrifices, and pulvinarian services shall be celebrated in such manner as the decurions determine and decree concerning the aforesaid matters -- to wit, the appointment of directors, the celebration of games in the circus, the superintendence of sacrifices, and the celebration of pulvinarian services. And whatever the decurions determine and decree concerning the aforesaid matters shall be legal and valid; and all the said persons, to whom such matter appertains and for whom it is proper in accordance with this law to perform any such matter, without malicious deception shall perform the same. If any person acts in contravention of this regulation, for every such act, he shall be condemned to pay to the colonists of the colony Genetiva Julia 10,000 sesterces and any of the colonists, at will, shall have the right and the power to bring an action, a claim, and a suit for that amount of

money, in accordance with this law, in a recuperatory action, before a duumvir or a prefect.

129. All duumvirs, aediles, and prefects of the colony Genetiva Julia, and likewise all decurions of the colony Genetiva Julia, diligently and without malicious deception, shall observe and obey the decrees of the decurions, and shall use their diligence to do and to perform, in a proper manner and without malicious deception, all things whatsoever it is proper a for the said persons respectively to do and to perform in accordance with the decree of the decurions. If any person fails so to act or with malice aforethought acts in contravention of this regulation, for every such act or omission he shall be condemned to pay to the colonists of the colony Genetiva Julia 10,000 sesterces and any of the colonists, at will, shall have the right and the power to bring an action, a claim, and a suit for that amount of money, in accordance with this law, in a recuperatory action, before a duumvir or a prefect.

130. No duumvir or aedile or prefect of the colony Genetiva Julia shall propose to the decurions of the colony Genetiva, or consult the decurions, or carry a decree of the decurions, or enter or order such decree to be entered in the public records, and no decurion when such matter is discussed shall declare a vote among the decurions, or frame a decree of the decurions, or enter or order such decree to be entered in the public records, whereby any senator of the Roman people, or the son of such senator. shall be adopted, chosen, or created patron of the colony Genetiva, unless three fourths of the decurions approve means of voting Tables and unless the person concerned, at the time when such matter is discussed, is a private person in Italy without imperium. If any person in contravention this regulation proposes to the decurions, or carries or causes to be carried a decree of the decurions, or enters or orders such decree to be entered in the public records, or if any person declares a vote among the decurions, or frames a decree of the decurions, or enters or orders such decree be entered in the public records, for every such act committed in contravention of this law he shall be condemned to pay to the colonists of the colony Genetiva Julia 100,000 sesterces and any of the colonists,

at will, shall have the right and the power to bring an action, a claim, and a for that amount of money, in accordance with this law, in a recuperatory action, before a duumvir or an interrex or a prefect.

131. No duumvir or aedile or prefect of the colony Genetiva Julia shall propose to the decurions of the colony Genetiva, or consult the decurions, or carry a decree of the decurions, or enter or order such decree to be entered in the public records, and no decurion shall declare a vote among the decurions, or frame a decree of the decurions, or enter or cause such decree to be entered in the public records, and no decurion shall declare a vote among the decurions, or frame a decree of the decurions, or enter or cause such decree to be entered in the public records, whereby any senator of the Roman people, or the son of such senator, shall be adopted as a public guest of the colony Genetiva Julia, or whereby the relation or the contract of public hospitality shall be concluded with any such person, unless a majority of the decurions approve by means of voting Tables and unless the person concerned, at the time when such matter is discussed, is a private person in Italy without imperium. If any person in contravention of this regulation, proposes to the decurions, or carries or causes to be carried a decree of the decurions, or enters or orders such decree to be entered in the public records, or if any person declares a vote among the decurions, or frames a decree of the decurions, or enters or

orders such decree to be entered in the public records, for every such act committed in contravention of this law he shall be condemned to pay to the colonists of the colony Genetiva Julia 10,000 sesterces and any of the colonists, at will, shall have the right and the power to bring an action, a claim, and a suit for that amount of money, in accordance with this law, in a recuperatory action, before a duumvir or a prefect.

132. No person in the colony Genetiva, being a candidate or standing for election to any magistracy within the colony Genetiva Julia, after the issuance of this law, in order to seek such magistracy, or during the year in which he is a candidate, or stands for or intends to stand for such magistracy with malice aforethought shall provide entertainments, or invite any person to dinner, or hold or provide a banquet, or with malice aforethought cause another person to hold a banquet or invite any person to dinner with a view to his candidature, but, nevertheless, the said candidate himself, who is seeking a magistracy, may invite, if he so desires, without malicious intent, during the said year daily any persons not exceeding nine. No candidate seeking office shall, with malice aforethought, give or make largess of any gift or present or any other thing with a view to his candidature. Nor any person, with a view to the candidature of another, shall provide entertainments, or invite any person to dinner, or hold a banquet, or, with malice aforethought, give or make largess of any gift or present or any other thing. If any person acts in contravention of this regulation, he shall be condemned to pay to the colonists of the colony Genetiva Julia 5,000 sesterces and any of the colonists, at will, shall

have the right and the power to bring an action, a claim, and a suit for that amount of money, in accordance with this law, in a recuperatory action, before a duumvir or a prefect."

133. Respecting all persons who are or shall be colonists of the colony Genetiva Julia: the wives of all such persons, being within the colony Genetiva Julia in accordance with this law, as well as their husbands, shall obey the laws of the colony Genetiva Julia and in all good faith shall enjoy in accordance with this law all such rights as are specified in this law.

134. No duumvir or aedile or prefect of the colony Genetiva after the issuance of this law shall propose to the decurions of the colony Genetiva, or consult the decurions, or carry a decree of the decurions, or enter or order such decree to be entered in the public records; and no decurion, when such matter is discussed, shall declare a vote among the decurions, or frame a decree of the decurions, or enter or cause such decree to be entered in the public records, whereby any public money or anything else shall be given or granted to any person, as a reward for holding office, or for giving or promising a gladiatorial show, or for the sake of giving or erecting a statue ...